1 MONTH OF
FREE
READING

at

www.ForgottenBooks.com

By purchasing this book you are eligible for one month membership to ForgottenBooks.com, giving you unlimited access to our entire collection of over 1,000,000 titles via our web site and mobile apps.

To claim your free month visit:

www.forgottenbooks.com/free514658

ISBN 978-0-260-91430-9
PIBN 10514658

STORE FRONTS IN TERRA COTTA

NATIONAL
TERRA COTTA SOCIETY
ONE MADISON AVENUE · NEW YORK
MEMBERS' FACTORIES IN ALL PARTS OF THE COUNTRY

HERE are some stores in every city that everybody knows. Almost always there is something unique and distinctive about such stores. Almost always they have the cream of the local trade. If you investigate, you will find that in a great many cities a large proportion of the newest of these well-known, successful stores have handsome fronts of Terra Cotta. It may be a beautiful touch of color that gives them such distinction. It may be a tasteful, ornamental design. But all over the country you will find that the very best work in store fronts is now being done in Terra Cotta.

It is not alone for store fronts that Terra Cotta has had such a remarkable development of recent years. From coast to coast Terra Cotta is now used on most of the newest and finest hotels and residences, office buildings and railroad stations, stores, schools, banks, theatres, moving picture houses, etc. In the following pages, however, we want to tell you more particularly about the advantages of Terra Cotta for store fronts, and to show you pictures of what progressive merchants in many lines of business have done to give their stores the bright, clean, distinctive appearance that attracts the best class of trade.

Terra Cotta has many unique advantages that make it the ideal permanent building material for store fronts. In the first place it gives wonderful opportunities for the use of color and ornament. Terra Cotta designs have a wide range, from the most elaborate and artistic treatments in rich colors to simple and dignified designs that are both beautiful and inexpensive.

Terra Cotta is an economical building material. The first cost is moderate, and there is no up-keep cost, such as painting or renovating. Glazed Terra Cotta can be washed clean with soap and water.

Terra Cotta is permanent, and because it is made by fire it is fireproof. It is unaffected by weather conditions in any climate and it never fades.

As an advertising proposition alone, a Terra Cotta store front is a profitable investment. It gives character and distinction to any store. The Terra Cotta store shines out by contrast with dull and dingy neighbors. It has the trim, neat appearance that fairly invites a customer in. It talks of quality goods and up-to-date service. It attracts the desirable new trade that is the breath of life to any business. If erected to rent, a Terra Cotta building is not likely to lack tenants.

As a means of putting new life into old properties, Terra Cotta is particularly valuable. Anyone who has had much experience with real estate investments knows how difficult it is to keep old properties occupied at a satisfactory rent. Terra Cotta works wonders in remodeling dingy, run-down buildings into attractive, easily rented stores and offices. As a real estate expert recently put it "the general character of the old building is entirely changed, and in its place we have a new style of building with a well-designed and interesting looking facade, whose white glazed Terra Cotta and spots of color will give it enough character and life to make it the show place of the neighborhood, and give it the first call on seeking tenants. 'The best place in the neighborhood' carries with it an advertising value which seldom fails."

Because of these many practical advantages, up-to-date architects everywhere favor the use of Terra Cotta for store fronts. It permits them to work out attractive color schemes and beautiful designs in the most effective and economical form. Builders like to work in Terra Cotta for similar reasons. They know that Terra Cotta is a dependable material that lets them deliver a building on schedule time to the complete satisfaction of the owner. No special machinery or apparatus is required, and any good builder can erect a Terra Cotta store front.

If you are interested in the possibilities of Terra Cotta and would like definite information in regard to a Terra Cotta front for your store, or for any building enterprise in which you are interested, write to us.

The National Terra Cotta Society is at your service. If you will tell us just what your building problem is, it is probable that we can offer some helpful suggestions.

In writing, address the NATIONAL TERRA COTTA SOCIETY, 1 MADISON AVENUE, NEW YORK CITY. You incur no obligation at all. We are anxious to help you find out anything you want to know about Terra Cotta. That is what the Society was organized to do.

The various members of this Society make Terra Cotta and sell it, but the National Terra Cotta Society has nothing to sell.

It is merely concerned that you should know the possibilities of Terra Cotta as a building material for your particular purposes.

In the following pages are shown photographs of a variety of Terra Cotta store fronts for many different lines of business, together with brief descriptions of color schemes, designs and decorative treatment. Following the photographs will be found a brief description of exactly what Terra Cotta is and how it is made.

S A N   F R A N C I S C O ' S   T E R R A   C O T T A   L I N E

ADAMS LAUNDRY, CHICAGO, ILL.

Architect—William H. Pruyn, Jr.

Pure white glazed Terra Cotta with delicately tinted ornamentation gives
just the right suggestion of immaculate cleanliness to this successful laundry

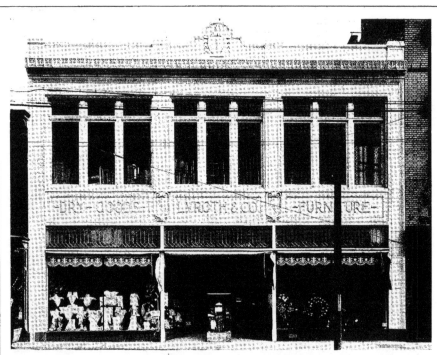

L. V. ROTH & CO., WEST NEW YORK, N. J.
Architect—William Mayer, Jr.

This typical design in dark cream matt glazed Terra Cotta shows economy of construction in the way the delicate modeling in low relief repeats frequently throughout the design. At the same time the effect, with letters of name panel in dark blue, is extremely rich and attractive.

C H I C A G O ' S   . T E R R A   C O T T A   L I N E

GHIRADELLI BUILDING, SAN FRANCISCO, CAL.
Architect—William Mooser

This beautiful building is convincing evidence that Terra Cotta is quite as effective in a simple,
restrained treatment as in ornamental designs. The finish is white matt glazed Terra Cotta.

MONITOR STORE, SPRINGFIELD, MASS.

Architect—H. A. Seabury

A simple and inexpensive treatment for a small store in white full-glazed Terra Cotta combined with rich coloring in blue and gold

MERCHANTS NATIONAL BANK, PORTLAND, ORE.

Architects—McNaughton & Raymond

Here we have an example of the use of Terra Cotta to give that atmosphere of
strength and dignity so desirable for buildings which house financial institutions.

KERSHAW & CROWL BUILDING, PHILADELPHIA, PA.

Architects—Savery, Scheltz & Savery

You would never guess that this attractive store building is a remodeled combination of two old dwellings. The front is of white glazed Terra Cotta.

STORE BUILDING, AUBURN, CAL.

Architect—Allen D. Fellows

An excellent architectural design in gray matt Terra Cotta showing the possibilities of this material for large store buildings

UNIVERSITY STATE BANK BUILDING, SEATTLE, WASH.

Architect—George Hughes

This handsome building gave a bank suitable quarters and, at the same time, proved a profitable investment with its easily rented stores and offices.

WINTEROTH & COMPANY, NEW YORK CITY

Architect—Fred Jaeger

Here again we see the distinctive effect of Terra Cotta construction. Notice
how this bright, clean store front shines by contrast with its neighbors.

STRATTON STORE BUILDING, COLORADO SPRINGS, COLORADO
Architects—McClaren & Thomas

Stores and offices in this distinctive building are always in demand. The decorative treatment is in light buff standard finish Terra Cotta

E. STINE & SON UNDERTAKING COMPANY, KANSAS CITY, MO.
Architects—McKecknie & Trask

A massive monumental effect in Terra Cotta of Missouri Red Granite finish gives an appropriate setting for an undertaking establishment.

STORE BUILDING, NEW HAVEN, CONN.
Architect—C. F. Townsend
Elaborate ornamentation combined with rich colors attracts the eyes of all passers-by to this distinctive store front

HAVERHILL ELECTRIC COMPANY BUILDING, HAVERHILL, MASS.
(Before rebuilding with Terra Cotta)
Architect—James T. Ball

The two photographs on these facing pages illustrate the possibility of transforming an old, ramshackle building into modern, attractive stores and offices by the use of architectural Terra Cotta. Such remodeling in Terra Cotta can be carried out without interruption to business

HAVERHILL ELECTRIC COMPANY BUILDING, HAVERHILL, MASS.
(After rebuilding with Terra Cotta)

This striking transformation was accomplished by the use of cream matt glazed Terra Cotta for the first story elevation, trim, cornice and parapet. At a very moderate expense an unprofitable investment was thus changed into a desirable, easily rented store and office building.

R. W. SAUNDERS, GLENS FALLS, N. Y.
Architect—Marcus T. Reynolds

A typical Terra Cotta design executed with an attractive color scheme in green,
yellow, blue and mart white. The whole effect gives an air of trim neatness.

FIRESTONE TIRE AND RUBBER COMPANY, LOS ANGELES, CAL.

Architects—Morgan, Walls & Morgan

This clean-cut front in cream matt glazed Terra Cotta helps to make this
one of the most successful automobile accessory stores in Los Angeles.

WIERSEMA BANK BUILDING, CHICAGO, ILL.

Architect—William G. Carnegie

A handsome decorative treatment in cream matt glazed and gray speckled
granite Terra Cotta made it easy to secure tenants for these stores and offices.

COHN STORE BUILDING, GREAT FALLS, MONTANA

Architect—George H. Shanley

A strong treatment in Terra Cotta of light gray granite tint with white panels gives distinction and character to this clothing store

SALOMON BUILDING, CHICAGO, ILL.

Architects—Lebenbaum & Marx

A beautiful treatment in cream enameled Terra Cotta proved an asset of great business value in securing desirable tenants for this store building

**FISKE BUILDING,
MINNEAPOLIS, MINN.**

Architect—Victor De Brauwere

Two panels in faience at top of building show St. Anthony Falls as they were at the time of discovery and as they are today. This is an excellent example of the possibilities of Terra Cotta in making a store unique and distinctive. The rest of the treatment is in cream matt glazed Terra Cotta with ivory tint mouldings.

INGLIS SHOP, WINNIPEG, MANITOBA
Architects—Ross & MacDonald

This is probably one of the best known tailor shops in the Northwest, and its handsome Terra Cotta front has helped to make it so. The finish is cream glazed Terra Cotta with letters in black.

J. A. RIGBY CIGAR COMPANY, MANSFIELD, OHIO

Architect—Vernon Redding

A beautiful treatment in cream matt glazed Terra
Cotta, marked by tasteful simplicity and restraint.

RITCHIE & CORNELL BUILDING,
NEW YORK CITY

Architect—James C. Green

An effective decorative treatment in Terra Cotta of granite
finish. Note the contrast between this attractive structure and
the building next door.

KRUGER'S, BALTIMORE, MD.

Architect—Walter M. Geiske

This extremely artistic effect is produced by a comparatively simple treatment in cream matt glazed Terra Cotta

WHITE AUTOMOBILE COMPANY, DENVER, COLO.

Architect—Robert A. Pierre

An excellent example of the suitability of Terra Cotta construction for automobile showrooms and garages. White matt glazed Terra Cotta with blue matt glazed panels surrounding the White Company's radiator emblem.

OGLEBAY STORES, KANSAS CITY, MO.

Architect—Edgar C. Faris

An attractive color scheme worked out in white and green matt glazed Terra Cotta gives beauty and distinction to these stores

P. H. RUEBEL & COMPANY, LITTLE ROCK, ARK.

Architects—Mann & Stern

The base course of this attractive store front is in Terra Cotta of a pink granite finish.
The remainder of the front shows an effective treatment in old ivory Terra Cotta.

A. R. DAVIS MOTOR COMPANY, CLEVELAND, OHIO
Architect—Frank D. Skeel

This trim building of cream glazed Terra Cotta, with base course in a pink granite glazed finish, houses the showrooms and garage of the Cleveland agent for the Studebaker Motor Car.

CHILDS RESTAURANT, NEW ORLEANS, LA.
Architect—Favrot & Livaudais

This simple, graceful front of Terra Cotta gives the right suggestion of appetizing cleanliness within.

THE EDISON SHOP, NEW YORK CITY
Architects—Shape & Brady

This well-known Fifth Avenue shop is a striking example of the artistic possibilities of Terra Cotta. The first story and side piers are of gray granite finish. The window trim is of matt cream and lustrous gold. The frieze is an effective combination of rich colors. The entire front is built of architectural Terra Cotta.

WENGLER & MANDELL, CHICAGO, ILL.
Architects—Mandie & Jensen

This treatment in full-glazed cream white Terra Cotta with name letters in black is an excellent
example of the dignified restraint that gives an unmistakable air of distinction to any building.

THOMPSON'S RESTAURANT, ST. LOUIS, MO.

Architects—Klipstein & Rathmann

A decorative treatment in Terra Cotta giving an inviting air of cleanliness which is worth real money to any dairy lunch. It should be remembered also that Terra Cotta can be washed clean with soap and water. Both the Thompson's and Childs' dairy lunch chains are extensive users of Terra Cotta fronts.

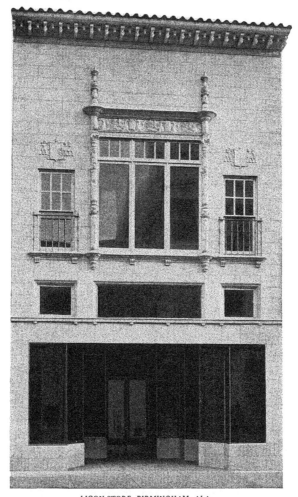

LIGON STORE, BIRMINGHAM, ALA.
Architect—W. C. Weston

This store front, entirely of old ivory matt glazed Terra Cotta,
combines delicacy and refinement with maximum attention value.

THE MAKING OF TERRA COTTA

Terra Cotta, as a literal translation of the Italian words indicate, is "Burnt Clay." Modern Terra Cotta is, of course, a more complex product and it undergoes many operations besides burning, but the basis of Terra Cotta is always clay and the final operation in its manufacture is always burning at a tremendous temperature.

Terra Cotta is a practically imperishable material. The earliest written records of mankind have come down to us on a crude form of burnt clay. Assyria, Phœnicia, Babylon, all show examples of Terra Cotta in its earliest architectural application; its development can be traced clearly through the southern countries of the Eastern hemisphere, in Egypt, Italy and Spain. In Italy, in the Fifteenth Century, Lucca Della Robbia executed much of his best work in Terra Cotta, and was particularly successful in the development of glazed colors. It has taken many years to attain and surpass the point at which he left the development of Terra Cotta.

In this country Architectural Terra Cotta was first manufactured shortly after 1870. Its improvement has been rapid. First used only for the ornament of a building and in the red and buff colors, it soon reached a point of structural efficiency that made it of great practical use. The successful development of the first glazes less than twenty years ago gave great impetus to further advance, for with the principle of Terra Cotta glazes understood the matter of developing various colors was comparatively simple. Today almost any color can be produced.

So in modern Architectural Terra Cotta we have a thoroughly practical structural material and one that is susceptible to treatment in any one color or any combination of soft or brilliant colors. Add to this the possibility of flexible modeling in a plastic state before burning, the fact that it is fireproof and economical to manufacture and erect, and the very general use of Architectural Terra Cotta is easily understood.

In the manufacture of Terra Cotta, models are made for every piece different in size and shape, and plaster moulds are made from the models. The fact that a large number of pieces may be pressed from one mould is largely responsible for the economy of Architectural Terra Cotta construction. The plastic Terra Cotta body is pressed in the mould by hand, and after turning out of the mould the piece is finished by hand. The pieces are then dried, and at this point the color glaze, or slip, is applied and the material placed in the kilns.

The kilns are fired to a heat at which the Terra Cotta is white hot, shimmering and translucent. The color develops by chemical reaction and the glaze vitrifies. Partial vitrification occurs in the Terra Cotta body, which takes on a flint-like hardness. It is this high temperature treatment that mades Terra Cotta fireproof.

From the kiln the Terra Cotta is taken to the fitting shops where it is assembled, inspected, and marked with the setting numbers, according to the setting drawings which the manufacturer prepares for the builder.

Terra Cotta is always carefully packed for shipment in hay or straw, and the loads braced with care. Upon arrival at the destination the builder has only to follow the manufacturer's construction drawings to erect the Terra Cotta in a thoroughly satisfactory manner.

Irving Underhill, N. Y.
©

N E W   Y O R K ' S   T E R R A   C O T T A   L I N E

Lightning Source UK Ltd.
Milton Keynes UK
UKHW010806211118
332624UK00007B/113/P